Contents

		Page
1	The Trouble with Max	1
2	Max's Great Idea	4
3	Gaming Heaven	9
4	Max Under Pressure	13
5	The Countdown Begins	15
6	Disaster Strikes	20
7	Game Over?	24

1

The Trouble with Max

'Max!'

Max didn't look up from the computer.
If he had heard, he didn't show it.

'Max – *quick*!'

It was his mum's voice.

Max tapped at the keyboard.
An explosion showed on his screen.

There was a loud crash from the kitchen.
After a pause,
Max's mum crashed into his room.

'Didn't you hear me?'

She sounded very angry, thought Max.
He didn't quite turn to look at her, though.
He couldn't risk
losing this part of the game.

'I did hear something…' he mumbled.

'I should think you did.
That was the shopping I was carrying.
I put a bag on the side
and it started to fall.
But I had my hands full of other bags.
I was trying to catch everything.
That's why I called you, to help.
Now a jar is cracked
and the eggs are broken!'

'Oh,' said Max.

He was finding it hard to listen *and* play.

'Is that all you can say? That stupid game!'
shouted his mum, really angry now.
'I have been at work, and done the shopping.
All you can do is play that all day.
You can at least help me clear up the mess.
I still have to cook tea, you know.'

'Um, sorry, yes, I'll clear it up.
Just give me five minutes to finish this,'
said Max.

'Five minutes?' asked his mum, crossly.
'I know your five minutes.
Well, tea will be late in that case.
I'm not starting it till the mess
is cleared up.'
And she stormed off.

2
Max's Great Idea

They sat together late that evening, eating.
Tea was more than an hour late.
Neither of them said very much.
This was because Max's mum was cross.
She thought Max was thinking about
how to apologise.
In fact, Max was thinking about his game.
He was planning how to get to the next level.

Max's mum picked up their plates.
Baggy, their old grey cat, mewed at her feet.
'You forgot to feed her again,'
said Max's mum.
'You spend too much time on that game.
I've told you before. It isn't healthy.'

'There's nothing else to do,' said Max.

'What about your friends?' asked his mum.
'You used to go round and see them.'

'They only play on the computer anyway.
We play together online.
Just at our own houses,' said Max.

'Can't you all go out together?'
asked his mum.

'To do what?' asked Max.
'Hang around, annoy people, drink and smoke?'

It was true, now she thought about it.
There wasn't much for young people in town.
There was a tennis court, she remembered.
And a football pitch on the park.
She didn't dare remind Max though.
She had to admit, he wasn't the sporty type.

'Well, you can help me more,' she said.
'I pay for that computer with my work.
You could earn the money for the internet.'

Max didn't like the sound of that.
Work at the supermarket,
as well as at school?
When would he have time to game?

'It wouldn't be so bad,
if you just played less.'
His mum was talking again.
'I don't see why
you have to do it *all* the time.
And you never get off quickly.
You get so angry if I need you for a moment.'

'I can't save it, you see,' said Max.
'If I lose the game, I go down the rankings.
I'm very high up now – tenth in the UK.'

Max's mum looked impressed for a moment.
Then she said, 'But what good is that?'

Max and his mum didn't have much money.
The computer had come from her old boyfriend.
His mum saved up money from her job.
She bought him games and extras for it.
She worked hard,
but they would never be rich.

Suddenly, Max had an idea.
It was better than the supermarket.

3
Gaming Heaven

———————————

'If you beat everyone,
you get a prize,' he said.

'Very likely,' said his mum, with a frown.
'Bring your mug as well. You can wash up.'

Max followed her to the kitchen.
'No, really.
You can see for yourself,' he said.

His mum started filling the sink.
She gave Max a gentle shove towards it.
Then she passed him some dirty plates.

'What prize?' she asked, picking up a cloth.

'A holiday in Malaysia. A four-wheel drive,'
said Max.

'A car too? I bet it's a trick,' said his mum.
She put a plate of cat food down for Baggy.

'A famous company is running it,' said Max.
'You can read about it online, if you want.'

'Well, I'll look when we've finished this,'
said his mum.

That evening, she read over Max's shoulder.
'It does sound alright,' she agreed.
'You come first in the UK online tournament.
Then you win the car and holiday.
After that, you battle in the world final.'

11

Max read the rules carefully with her.
'Malaysia is where the battle takes place.
So really, the holiday is just for that.'

'But you win two tickets,' said his mum.
'So I would be there to keep an eye on you.
And you win the car.'

'I'm not old enough to drive yet,' said Max.
'It says here,
the car goes to a responsible adult.'

'That's me, alright,' said his mum.

4
Max Under Pressure

'There's just one thing,' said Max, worried.
'I'm only ranked tenth at the moment.'

'They see who is number one in three weeks,'
said Max's mum.
'You're always saying you are good.
Can you do it?'

She looked at Max.
He looked back at her.

'I think so, but I'd have to play all the time.'

Max's mum blew the hair out of her eyes.

'I'd go for it,' she said, 'but properly.'

'Alright then,' said Max.

He felt strange, important, a bit scared.
He liked to get the highest ranking he could.
He liked to play as much as possible.
He *was* good.
So why was he worried?

5
The Countdown Begins

The next three weeks were very busy for Max.
There were no holidays during this time.
Max had to do most of his homework
while at school.
This gave him time to game in the evenings.

'This is hard,' he admitted to his mum.
'Other people seem to be on all day,
but I have to battle after school
to keep my place.'

Now he found there was no time to watch TV.
He had to game as soon as he got in.
He paused for tea, but played until bedtime.

When he slept, the game went on in his head.
Then as he rose through the levels,
it got harder.

At the end of the first week, he was seventh.
'That's good,' said his mum when he told her.
She picked up Baggy and went off to watch TV.
He heard her laughing at a comedy.
He was too tired to watch.
He had to finish the game, then go to bed.

That weekend,
one of his friends, Jamie, called.
'Are you coming out?' he asked.
'I'm taking the dinghy to the river.'

'Didn't we lose the oars last time?'
asked Max.

Jamie shrugged.
'Well, we could use planks or something.'

'Can't,' said Max, 'Sorry. I'm seventh.
I have to be number one in two weeks.'

'Number one what?' asked Jamie, puzzled.

'War Demon Online,' said Max.

'Oh, that,' said Jamie,
'I don't play any more.
Well done, though. Cool. See you.'

Later, Max imagined the fun in the dinghy.
Which friends would be there?
But he had no time to think of those things.

Halfway through the second week, Baggy died.
Max's mum found the old cat, curled up.
At first she thought she was asleep.

Max felt guilty.
He had passed Baggy without a glance earlier.
He had been on his way to the computer.
Baggy had been there before he was born.
He couldn't imagine their house without her.

They buried her in the garden.
Max's mum cried.
Max's eyes were a bit wet but he dried them.
He hadn't time.
He had to get back to the game.

6
Disaster Strikes

It was part way through week three.
Max, known as Destroyer, was in second place.
He was very tired, but playing very well.
Online, on the game, he was almost famous.
People had noticed him.

Skyrider, the number one, was older than him.
This person seemed to play all day.
So Max had started to get up very early.
He played before school.
By playing straight after school,
he caught up.

His head was full of the battles.
At break and lunch times he did homework.
This meant he couldn't chat with his friends.
Even then, teachers moaned his work was poor.

On that Wednesday evening, it all went wrong.
He tried to fix the computer.
He wanted to make it faster.
The whole thing crashed.
When he switched it on,
a blue screen came up.
He tried again and again.
An hour and a half had passed already.
He knew Skyrider would be number one.

How many places would he have fallen?
He only had two days left.
All of this would have been for nothing.

Max's mum heard him shouting and stamping.
She looked in to see what was wrong.
Max had tears in his eyes.

'I'll phone someone,' she said quickly.
Max knew a repair person would cost money.
They had never called one before.
Somehow Max had always fixed it.
His shoulders sagged.

He could hear his mum talking on the phone.
Then she came back, looking pale.
'No-one can come out until tomorrow,' she said.

'Then I've lost,' said Max.

'But you've got till midday Saturday!'
said his Mum.

'The others will be too far ahead
by then,' said Max.
His mum put her hands through her hair.
'I wish I knew someone who did computers.'

Max thought for a moment.
Jamie was good.
Jamie's dad was even better.
But he hadn't done much for Jamie lately.
Jamie had every right
to tell him to get lost.

Much as he didn't want to, he made the call.
This was too important.

7
Game Over?

Max could hardly take in what had happened.
He remembered the last blow he'd struck.
Then he'd stared at the score on the screen.
Skyrider was finished.
Destroyer had won through to the final.

His mum had jumped about and screamed.
But Max had just wanted to go to bed.

Now, two weeks later, here they were.
Thanks to Jamie and his Dad, he thought.
They had worked for ages on the computer.

Penang was very hot.
He hadn't seen much of it yet.
The final was being held at a college.
It looked just like a building from home.

Mum kissed his cheek for luck.
'I'm off to look at the shops,' she smiled.
'See you back at the hotel afterwards.'

They had won the holiday.
They had won the four-wheel drive.
If Max won this final, the prize was money.

He was very tired.
He didn't feel as if he'd slept for weeks.
The flight to Malaysia had worn him out.
Mum was very happy.
She had told him that she didn't mind
whether he won or not.

That evening,
a taxi dropped Max back at the hotel.
Mum gave him a hug.
She was tanned already.
She wore sparkly earrings.
She had had her nails and hair done.

26

Max looked terrible.
His skin looked grey
from being inside for days.
He had dark lines under his eyes.

'I didn't win,' he said, 'It was too hard.'
He thought, but didn't say,
'and I didn't care any more.'

'It doesn't matter,' said his mum.
'I am very proud of you.
I'm going to sell the four-wheel drive.
I'll buy a cheaper car I can afford to run.
I will put the rest of the money in the bank.
You can use it towards your future.
A car for work, or a flat of your own.
But you should have a special present.'

Max's mum paused.
'I thought I would buy you a new computer.
A faster one, better for gaming.
What do you think?'
She smiled, and looked for his smile.

Max said, to her surprise:
'Thanks, Mum, but please don't bother.
I never want to look at a computer again.'

'There is one thing you could buy me though,'
Max added, stretching in his chair.

'What's that?' she asked.

'A pair of oars,' he said.

And before she could ask why,
he fell asleep at the table.